BODY TALK

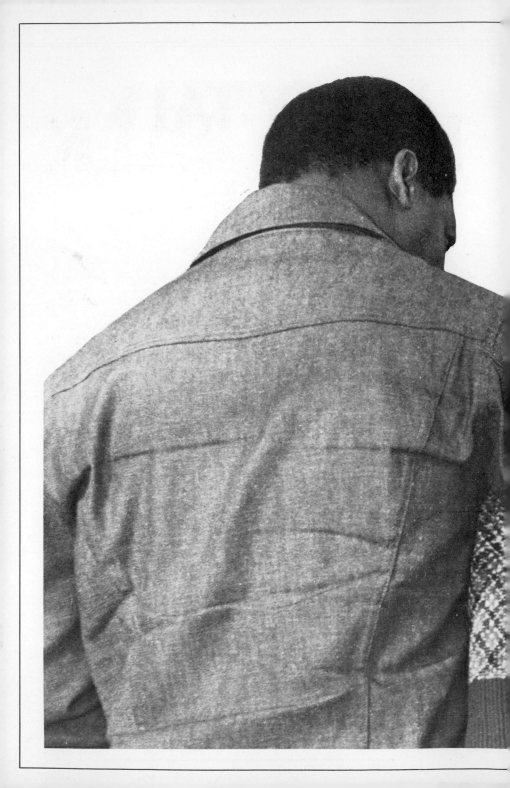

KATHLYN GAY

BODY TALK

PHOTOGRAPHS BY DAVID SASSMAN

CHARLES SCRIBNER'S SONS
NEW YORK

To Doris

*who also likes to people-watch, and
has shared her observations with me.*

CONTENTS

BODY TALK

ONE
"ACTIONS SPEAK LOUDER THAN WORDS"

Thump down the stairs and shuffle across the family room in your house. Plop onto a chair, then slide yourself down until the end of your spine is balanced on the edge of the seat. Slouch that way, with your arms crossed and your lips pressed tightly together. Lower your eyes and stare at your crossed arms. Pay no attention to anyone else in your household. Do not speak during the few minutes it takes to perform these actions.

If members of your family watch this silent performance, your father might growl: "Hey, shape up! You have to get ready for school whether you like it or not!"

Or your mother might ask: "What's wrong? Don't you feel well?"

A younger sister or brother might tease: "You are mad and I am glad. . . ."

Even though you did not speak a single word, each member of your family received some kind of message. Your father decided you didn't want to go to school. Your mother thought you were sick. And to a sister or brother it would seem you were angry about something.

So who would be right?

Maybe none of your family or maybe each of them picked up one small part of your message.

With your silent actions you could have been saying you didn't want to talk to anyone that morning. Possibly you woke up with a headache. You got out of bed and couldn't find the right clothes to wear. Then you really were upset and angry. Whatever the case, you would hardly have to explain how you felt because your actions had "spoken" for you. You had shown that something was definitely wrong, or at least not quite in balance.

The point is, without ever uttering a sound, a person can say all kinds of things with body positions (or postures) and movements (or gestures). A person "speaks" with facial expressions—the variety of ways the eyes and mouth move or the forehead wrinkles. A person "talks" by using certain hand and arm gestures. The way a person holds his head, the way he walks, sits, or stands—various parts of the body moving separately or together—sends messages to an observer.

Often words and actions are used at the same time to put across messages. Suppose your family moves into a new neighborhood. The first time you meet other young people on the block, you would want to get acquainted. If you asked to join a game or walk with the other kids to a neighborhood store, you might smile a lot (without ever realizing it). You could share part of a candy bar as you talk to a stranger. Your words *and* gestures say "I'm friendly." Possibly you'd toss a ball out to one of the neighborhood kids. You would hold your hands up to catch the ball on a return throw. Not only your words but your actions also would say: "I'd like you to throw the ball and let me be part of your fun."

Psychiatrists, social scientists, anthropologists, and others who study human behavior point out that the gesture—which can be almost any motion of the body—was probably the first form of human speech. The experts also tell us that the hands and face are the most natural parts of the body to use

Many types of body language and gestures are learned at an early age. Here a toddler responds to the open-arms gesture, which is a silent message for "come here," understood by almost everyone.

for gestures. Almost everyone begins very early in life to communicate with some kind of body movement.

In fact, without realizing it, all of us learn a body language as well as a language that is verbalized, or spoken. Young children, for example, copy various kinds of behavior or learn the meaning of a gesture by seeing it over and over again in a particular situation. The up-and-down or the back-and-forth movements of the head are gestures taught even to babies. They soon realize that the nod means "yes" and the shake of the head is a "no."

Then, too, you've seen grown-ups teach youngsters how to

wave or to point. These actions are repeated and explained with directives like "say bye-bye" or "show us the kitty." Toddlers often mimic older brothers or sisters in a family. Did you ever see a little guy stand with his feet spread apart, his hands clenched in fists on his hips, his chin jutting out—an exact miniature of a big brother who is arguing or

Most of us are not aware of all the body movements, gestures, facial expressions, and postures we learn through modeling or copying the behavior of others. Young children, for example, often mimic the actions of older brothers or sisters. They learn not only useful skills, such as how to dress and groom themselves, but also how to sit, stand, walk, and other actions for specific situations.

defying someone? Many young children also copy actions by modeling themselves after older children on the school playground, in the halls, or at assemblies.

Some types of gestures, like the handshake, may have originated centuries ago. One story telling how the handshake began describes a knight in armor traveling by horseback through a deserted wood. He sees another knight in the distance coming toward him. Quickly, the first knight shifts his sword from his right hand to his left and raises his right hand high to show the approaching knight that his weapon hand is empty. That gesture, saying "Look, I'm unarmed and friendly," has finally come to be the greeting we know—reaching out an arm to another person, grasping that person's hand and shaking it.

Other types of body language may be instinctive. That is, people seem to do "what comes naturally." As Charles Darwin, the famous naturalist, once explained it: Even before children can talk they express anger by biting. He compared this action to that of young crocodiles "who snap their little jaws as soon as they emerge from the egg."

The smile is another action that is basic to almost all peoples. Often it means that the person who is smiling is feeling some kind of pleasure. But some smiles say "I'm embarrassed" or "I'm shy" or "Get away from me because I'm feeling uptight." A fake smile says "I don't think that's so funny!"

People reinforce or support the words they use with many kinds of body language. Gestures dramatize what a person actually says. For example, a hug from a grown-up who at the same time is telling you, "I'm sorry you were hurt," can really make you feel the grown-up's sincerity. The words express sympathy, but combined with the gesture you are bound to feel comforted.

In the same way, a frown on a person's face along with harsh words make it quite clear that anger, annoyance, or irritation is being expressed. Or how about seeing a person with clenched fists, lips tight, waiting to get a flu shot from a nurse? If that person says he's worried or scared, there's no doubt about it. You believe him. His gestures and actions support what he says.

You may not be aware of all the many kinds of gestures that accompany verbal forms of communication. But just about everyone has had the experience of trying to give someone else directions on how to get to a certain place. It's difficult to do without the use of one's hands and arms. Suppose you want to describe a monster movie. Could you do it without gestures? What happens when you want to let someone know you have a stomach ache? Usually, you clutch your middle as you give a verbal explanation about where you hurt. Try describing some exciting event like a great football play or the thrill of a carnival ride. During the recital, dozens of different gestures may be used to show as well as tell.

In recent years, a few behavior experts have begun to study body language in a scientific manner. This study, called *kinesics,* involves many procedures, such as observing people, filming their behavior, recording their actions. Everything from a blink of the eye to a wiggle of a foot is analyzed and categorized. These body movements are part of a special kind of language that can—with or without verbal speech—indicate fear, sadness, joy, anger, confusion, worry, and other emotions. In addition, through kinesics scientists

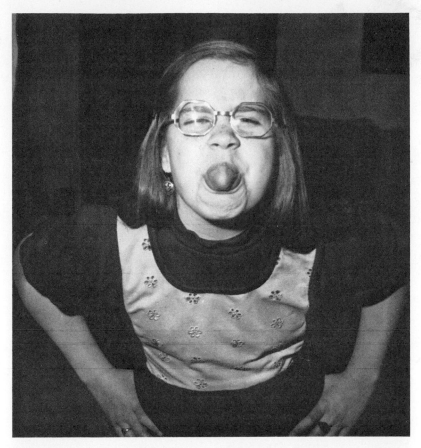

You won't need an explanation for this one. Who hasn't "made faces" as a silent message for "I'm mad at you!"

learn about people's attitudes. Body movements might tell how a person thinks or what he wants.

Actually, kinesicists (those who research various forms of body movements) study all forms of communication but they concentrate on visible behavior. They believe it is impossible to separate body movements or actions from verbal com-

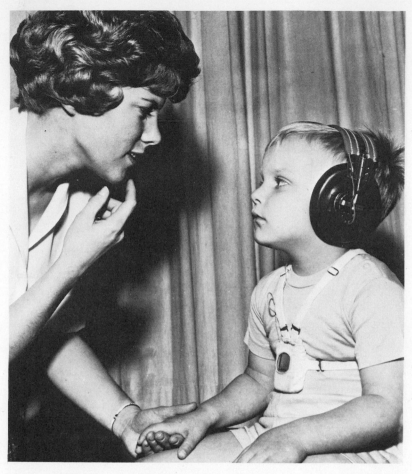

Young children who have hearing handicaps need help to learn how to speak. Along with some mechanical methods, various types of body language (gestures, touch, facial expressions) are used by therapists to help children overcome such disabilities. Photo courtesy United Way

munication. Dr. Ray Birdwhistell, a well-known kinesicist, points out that speech is used to express only 35 percent of what a person *really* feels or means. Gestures and body postures and positions can more honestly tell about our feelings and thoughts. And many times a person sends out a message with body movements that is the direct opposite of what he is saying with words.

Maybe you have been in a situtation where you've seen a classmate destroy property. Or you discovered a friend was shoplifting. If you were questioned later about either of these incidents you might want to protect your classmate or friend by saying, "I don't know anything about what happened."

Somehow, though, the person questioning is not fooled. Your eyes might drop in such a way that you are really saying, "Yes, I know what went on." Without your being aware of it, maybe your head nods slowly up and down in a "yes" signal.

You can probably think of other examples of the way gestures contradict the spoken words. There is the person who says he doesn't want any friends, but he always seems to demand attention by hitting, poking, shoving, or using other behavior that says "Notice me!"

On the other hand, members of a group might insist they are open to strangers. They say they'd like others to join in their fun or be a part of their group activities. Yet, some members might fold their arms and others turn partially away from an "outsider." Some faces might be set rigidly with tight lips, eyes staring straight ahead, and chins jutting out. In this case, group members would be using gestures or body movements that clearly state: "We don't want anyone else in our group. Leave us alone. Go away."

In certain situations, body signals and movements are easy to interpret, or "read." But in order to understand most silent messages you need to see the *whole* picture and hear what is being said too. Just because a person folds his arms tightly across his chest does not *always* mean "I'm closed up—don't come near me." Sometimes that gesture can be saying to others, "I'm really shy. I want to get to know you, but I can't get out of my shell."

Those who study body language have to put all the signals and movements together. Experts in kinesics would look not only at the crossed-arms gesture, but also might note the way a person holds his head. Is it thrown back or drooping? What about the eyes? Do they drop quickly or meet a gaze? What is the person saying with his shoulders? How is he standing or sitting? Are some actions and gestures deliberate? Have they been planned? Is the person aware of what he is doing? Or does he use gestures without conscious thought?

The spoken language must be noted too. Is the voice soft or loud? What is the speech pattern? Is the tone of voice or the pitch saying more than the words themselves?

Along with all this, body language experts study what is happening around a person. What does he do with space? Is there a lot of distance between the person being watched and others in the room? Or are people close together? Is there a large crowd or only a few people?

During the lunch hour, a young fellow approaches a couple of girls outside the school to join their conversation. The facial expressions and body postures of all three people indicate some self-consciousness or shyness. But once they begin to verbalize, or exchange spoken messages, they also show with body talk, or silent messages, that they will begin to "open up," or exhibit friendly behavior. For example, the young man's arms begin to move and raise up as he prepares to gesture and to support his verbal message. More relaxed smiles appear on the boy's and one of the girl's faces.

As you have probably guessed by now, many movements and expressions must be observed *in context,* or as they happen in a certain order. Conclusions cannot be drawn from a single smile, a nod, a wink, or a shrug. Such gestures are meaningful only as they relate to others' actions and the surrounding environment.

Yet, through the science of kinesics, many different kinds of body movements and gestures are being isolated and identified. For example, Dr. Birdwhistell has categorized hundreds of separate body movements and has created picture symbols, called *kinegraphs,* to represent them. A British research team recently described a variety of face, head, and body gestures, among them nine distinct kinds of smiles. Three of these are very common and they have been labeled the *simple smile* (the mouth slightly turned up at the edges with lips still together); the *upper smile* (like you do when you're happily greeting a friend or parents); and the *broad smile* (used at play or for the "big funny").

Still other researchers analyze gestures by *clusters*—sets of body movements that have certain meanings. They list some of these in categories like "boredom gestures" or "cooperative gestures." Different body movements fit together like words in a sentence or parts of a puzzle. They make a full picture, or cluster, that has meaning.

This type of knowledge is being used by psychiatrists, sociologists, and others who study the way people interrelate—how we get along and what keeps us apart.

An understanding of kinesics is also useful for businessmen, actors, speakers, teachers, and many others who lead, entertain, or guide groups. In addition, many individuals want to learn about body language and the meanings of movements in order to better understand themselves and those around them.

While it would take a great deal of study to become an expert on the subject, it does not require scientific background to be *aware* of body language. Almost everyone can discover how to read or use some of the silent messages described in this chapter. To develop the ability, you can observe the actions of people around you—your friends, relatives, members of your immediate family, classmates, and so on. You can also become aware of what you do with your body—what gestures and movements you use and how these communicate to others.

As you begin to notice specific body movements, you will also develop a curiosity about their meanings. Some of these will be discussed later on. But right now, take a first step toward understanding visible behavior or the silent messages of body language by checking out some common hand signs, arm signals, and body positions. Many are used so often you might not think of them as part of a "vocabulary." Yet, these silent signs and signals communicate important messages all the time.

TWO
SIGNS, SIGNALS, AND CEREMONIES

As mentioned earlier, one of the first hand or arm signals you learned was a wave to say "good-bye." And you found out very quickly that a pointing finger could say you wanted something. You learned a raised finger to the lips is the signal for "quiet." At an early age, you learned, too, that a policeman's raised hand means "stop" in traffic. This same signal, you discovered, has a different meaning in the classroom. There it tells the teacher you want to be noticed or you have the answer to a question.

During your school years you absorb various kinds of signs and signals that become part of your nonverbal vocabulary. If you want to say you respect the flag of your country, you put a hand over your heart or salute. If you are involved in sports, or just like to watch athletic contests, you know a number of signals that are part of different games. In baseball, the umpire's jerk of a thumb back over his shoulder means "You're out!" In basketball, a referee rolls his hands to signal a "traveling" violation. And in football, when the referee uses his right hand to hit the back of his leg at the bend of the knee, he is signaling that a player has hit an opponent from behind—a violation called "clipping."

At concerts, you know that a band leader's raised baton indicates that the musicians should get ready to play. On a bicycle you use hand signals to tell others on the road which way you are turning or to warn that you will stop.

In daily conversation, you are liable to use a great many

*A variety of hand signals are used on the job in a scrap metal yard.
Here, a pointing of the thumb to the ground directs the crane
operator to drop the load of scrap from the magnet.* Photo courtesy
Bob Lindahl

SIGNS, SIGNALS, AND CEREMONIES

signs and signals. You might scratch your head to indicate confusion. Beckoning with your index finger could mean "Come here." If you want to fight, raised fists say so without words. You pinch your nose with your fingers if you want to say "It stinks!" Pat the upper part of your leg and a pet dog may come running up to you. Use your thumb and finger to form a circle and you're saying "Great!" or "Perfect!" or "Job well done."

Hand and arm gestures are commonly used to communicate on many jobs. Hand signals get across messages when a person's voice cannot be heard because of noise or distance.

Take construction work. A foreman on a project might want to talk to the crane operator who is sitting in a cab high above the ground. With his left hand cupped slightly, fingers up under the outstretched palm of his right hand, a foreman signals to the crane operator to "Hoist hook slowly." Or a man in a deep hole can direct the operations of a huge scoop shovel by signaling, with sweeping motions of his hands and arms, that the hole should be wider.

At the Chicago Board of Trade, where thousands of bushels of grains or other commodities are bought and sold in a brief period each day, Monday through Friday, business is conducted at a frantic pace. Hundreds of brokers (those who buy and sell the commodities) shout their bids, phones ring, messengers rush to and fro, and electronic boards continually click and light up. There would be mass confusion if it were not for the system of hand signals brokers use to show how they are trading.

For example, a raised hand with the palm out means a broker wants to sell; the palm in means he's buying. Certain positions of the fingers, held horizontally, tell the fractions of cents for which the broker will trade.

At an airport, hand signals are used by mechanics to guide pilots while they park planes. On piers, a deckman signals directions to boom operators for loading and unloading cargoes from ships.

In a television studio, a stage manager uses arm and hand signals to send a variety of messages to people performing in front of the cameras. For one signal, the right arm is bent at the elbow and the hand forms a fist; the left arm crosses behind the right arm with the left hand also forming a fist. It may look like the stage manager has mixed up a boxing stance. But the signal merely means "Half a minute is left in the show."

If you have ever watched a deaf person use sign language, you know how important hand and arm gestures are to those

On many jobs, hand and arm signals are essential for communication. At the Chicago Board of Trade, thousands of bushels of grains and commodities such as lumber and soybean oil are sold through a system of hand signals. Each position of the fingers and hand indicates whether a broker is buying or selling a commodity and the fraction of a cent per unit for which he will trade.

| buy | 1/8 cent | 1/4 cent | 3/8 cent | 1/2 cent |
| sell | 5/8 cent | 3/4 cent | 7/8 cent | full cent |

with hearing handicaps. In the sign talk of the deaf, rapid hand and arm movements near different parts of the face and body have specific meanings. Unless you understand sign language, you cannot tell when one sign ends and another begins. They all seem to run together. But people with hearing handicaps who use sign language can distinguish the silent phrases and words that help them communicate. Some deaf people can "sing" songs in sign language or create poems. Humorous stories and jokes are told in sign language.

While sign language of all types is very expressive, it is not always constructive or helpful. Sometimes teasing insults are put across with head or facial gestures combined with arm or hand signals. Twirl an index finger beside your head and then point to another person. What are you saying? The other guy is crazy-mixed-up!

Place your hands on your hips and stick out your tongue. You know that one. The gesture could mean anything from "You're a dope" to "I'm mad at you." If you wrinkle your nose and make a motion by shoving your thumbs down toward the ground, you can say you don't like something. A thumb stuck on the end of the nose with fingers waving is a form of insult and a raised middle finger is highly insulting.

On a more positive note, sign language and signals make our everyday communication livelier and more interesting. And many signals have a variety of meanings. Take the outstretched or raised arm with a fist. It signals "Black Power." But the power sign is also a way to greet a brother, or it means "Hey, I'm with you" or "I support your cause." The signal has been adopted by many in political campaigns and by athletic teams to say "We're going to win."

Slang phrases, too, can be communicated with sign lan-

guage. Suppose you are in a heated conversation with someone. You could be arguing with a classmate about sports or
politics. The longer you argue, the higher your voice rises.
Your body may begin to dramatize your words with gestures
that show your anger—arms tensing, hands rigid as you try
to make your points. Then suddenly a third person comes
into the picture. A friend is signaling to you from across the
room. Body bent just slightly at the waist, his arms outstretched, he is crossing his arms in front of him, waving
them parallel to the floor.

What's he trying to tell you? Yeah, man, cool it!

Signs and signals also make it easier to communicate in
school or home situations.

Look in on the Bender family at dinner for a minute. There
isn't much conversation. Everybody is busy eating. Six-year-
old Tim reaches across the table for the bread. His father
looks up from his plate and gives Tim's hand a slight slap.
Tim gets the message. "Pass the bread, please," he says.

During the meal, Tim's older brother, Phil, asks for salt by
jabbing a finger in the direction of the shaker. While passing
the salt, Mrs. Bender frowns; Phil knows his mother doesn't
like pointing. But he shrugs and grins. (What's that mean? It
could be "So what?" or "Sorry, I forgot my table man-
ners.")

When he leans back in his chair, Mr. Bender signals without words that he has finished his meal. And the wiggling,
squirming body of Tim Bender says clearly that he is anxious
to leave the table.

This simplified example shows only a few common gestures that provide instant communication in a family. But
common signs and signals are used in special ways by indi-

People use various types of hand signals to greet each other, to show friendliness, or as a means of competition. Can you identify what the hands and arms signify in each of these?

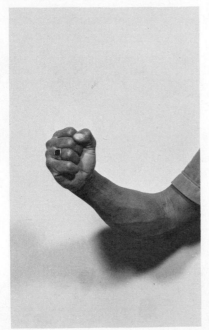

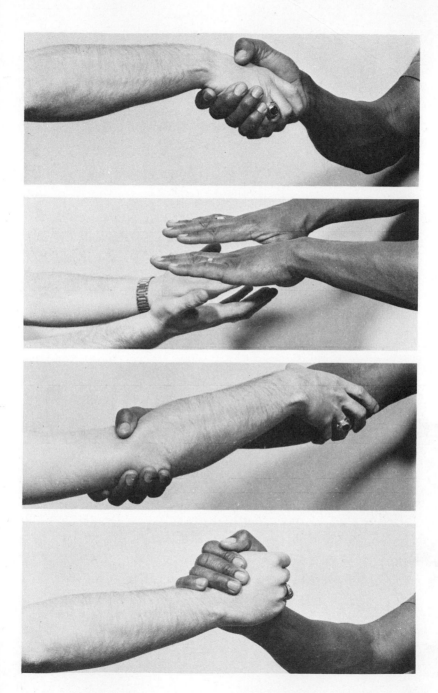

viduals too. Each member understands what the other is saying with particular gestures. For example, in one household, a mother's slow tap of her fingers on a table could mean she's angry. In another situation, though, that same gesture could say "Hmmm, I'm thinking" or "Something is worrying me."

Most of us learn our friends' special gestures too. In turn, our gestures are read by them. Do you scratch your nose when you are shy or embarrassed? Does your friend use a hands-on-hips gesture to say "Look. I'm going to speak"? Many times gestures alone can tell you whether your friend is cocky, sad, tired, lonely, happy, angry, or worried. You know because you have unconsciously absorbed many things about this person over a period of time.

Even among strangers there are common gestures easily understood by everyone. Sometimes these silent messages are part of formal ceremonies, such as religious services, weddings, funerals, or public events. After a play or some other type of entertainment, for instance, an audience participates in a custom that says without words "We enjoyed the performance" or "Great show." Of course you know that group gesture: a round of applause. At the same time, an actor, actress, or other performer can say "Thank you" with a bow.

At the start of many public events, when the national anthem is played or the flag is paraded, an audience stands as a sign of respect or show of loyalty to the country. At a rally or large gathering a speaker may come to the platform and raise his arms. This indicates he is ready to speak and the audience should be silent.

During religious ceremonies or rituals, body gestures and

hand signs speak reverently. Catholics make the "sign of the cross" when entering their church and genuflect (bend the knees) or drop to a kneeling position at various times during a service. A priest or a Protestant minister may raise his arms over his head when he wants to indicate a time of prayer. In a Jewish synagogue, or temple, one particularly important gesture involves the entire congregation. All rise in respect when the Ark is opened to remove the Torah, or Holy Scriptures, for reading.

In some religious groups around the country and in other parts of the world, various forms of bowing are used. This gesture in the Muslim faith is an elaborate ritual requiring many steps. The bowing ritual is used for prayer five times a

Bicycle safety also requires the use of hand signals, as shown here and on the following page. Here, the boy is showing that he intends to make a right turn.

SIGNS, SIGNALS, AND CEREMONIES

Other hand signals for bicycle safety include the signal to indicate a left turn (above) and a stop (left).

day and it includes facing toward Mecca (the holy city), kneeling, bending forward, and a complete prostration (lying face down).

Silent signs and signals are a part of almost every aspect of living—from religion to sports, from family gatherings to meetings with strangers, from business to pleasure. Most hand and arm signals are simple to learn. And ceremonial gestures, too, are easily understood if they are part of your particular way of life.

Yet there are subtle differences in body language. And you need to know the special ways each part of the body can talk before you can tell whether you are correctly reading a silent message.

THREE
THE "EYES" HAVE IT

Melissa looked her mother *straight in the eye* and explained what had happened.

Sean watched the other boys *from the corner of his eye.*

The two children *stared at their feet* and did not speak to their father.

Larry *winked* at her and grinned.

Barbara *glanced* at the crippled girl and *quickly looked away.*

The boy *stared* at the little man until the man whirled and angrily walked away.

They could see the old woman *peering* from between the curtains.

The teacher frowned as he *squinted* over his glasses and picked up the report on his desk.

All of the above statements have one thing in common. Each tells about some way the eyes were used to send silent messages.

Did you decide Melissa was honest or direct?

Was Sean suspicious or a bit wary of the other boys?

The children who stared at their feet could have been guilty of some mischief—right?

Maybe Larry was teasing or flirting.

And perhaps you decided Barbara was being thoughtful or showing respect by *not* looking too long at a person's handicap. Just the opposite was probably true of the boy who stared at the little man.

Was the peering old woman poking into someone else's business or just a bit curious? Is the teacher's squint a sign of poor eyesight or is he displeased with the report?

Eye movements and other facial expressions, like a smile or frown, plus head gestures, are the most noticed of all visible behavior. We look at each other's faces more than we look at other parts of the body, so we quickly learn meanings of eye contact (or lack of it) and other movements of the face and head. Sometimes these actions must be isolated or separated from others in order to develop awareness and to study body language. However, as with any kind of gesture, a wink, look, squint, nod, smile, or wrinkled forehead means little by itself.

Suppose you want to analyze a wink. Does that gesture *always* mean a person is teasing or has no serious intent? What about this situation:

A young man is leaning against a building, his arms crossed in front of him. His head is down with his chin practically resting on his chest. The brim of his hat is pulled down over his eyes. But he is watching people go by. Soon another man appears and, as he passes, the young man winks deliberately. After a few seconds he follows the other man and meets him around the other side of the building.

Now, what have you decided about the wink? In this instance, you might have concluded the young man was sinister, a shifty, sly character. And the wink was a sort of code or signal.

But change the scene a little. What if the people passing are pretty girls and the young man winks? Would the wink have another meaning? If friends gather around and the young man winks as he tells a story, what does the gesture mean then?

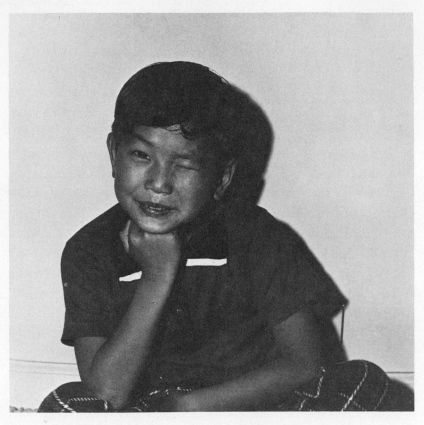

The wink has dozens—even hundreds—of different meanings but sometimes can be just a fun way to say "Hi!"

Once again, a single gesture can only be understood in context—as it is used with other body movements and within a certain setting.

If you have never thought about eye behavior or any other body movements before, you will at least have been aware of the *stare*. That is one type of body language that generally causes reactions and means the same thing to the majority of people in this country. The silent message you would send to another person with your stare is usually "You are odd or different" or "I'm angry and/or I'm challenging you."

Naturally that kind of message can cause problems. Just think about how you feel when someone stares at you. Unless you are performing or showing off, you get uncomfortable. Being stared at might make you feel self-conscious, sure that you are doing something wrong or that you look funny. You might get annoyed or mad.

Because of these kinds of reactions, parents often instruct their children *not* to stare. However, there are times when grown-ups or young people want to show their disapproval or dislike. So they deliberately look at others for long periods of time.

Suppose a grown-up stares at a teenage boy on the street who is not dressed or groomed to the adult's taste. The adult might even let his eyes move up and down, obviously taking in everything about the young man. It's no wonder the teenager reacts with: "What're *you* lookin' at, bud?" He resents the once-over. The stare makes him feel less than human.

There is a difference, though, in what people think a stare *is*. In middle-class American way of life, most strangers do not look at each other for any longer than a second at a time. They may glance at each other now and again, but if someone looks any longer than a second it is considered rude or a "put down." People from other countries and cultures have different ideas.

Arabs, for example, often look at others on the street for several seconds or minutes at a time without dropping their gaze. This would be insulting to an American.

If you visited in Israel, you might be upset by the way

Israelis look people up and down; you'd be sure people were staring at you. But Israelis would think no such thing. They are merely showing interest.

Cultural groups in the United States also have different opinions on when someone is staring and when he is not. In some black families, there is not as much eye contact as in most white families. Thus, some blacks feel that whites are staring at them if there is direct eye contact. And some whites think blacks are acting suspiciously if eye contact is avoided.

What this amounts to is that eye behavior, as with other gestures, can reflect one's culture or way of life. One could have Body English, or Body French, or Body Italian. Or a person might exhibit Black Body Talk or Yiddish Behavior and so on.

Just as it's difficult to define exactly what a stare is, it is no simple matter to describe the differences between "looks." A steady look can be a sign of interest, attention, or concern. People tend to look more often and longer at things or people they like than at those they dislike. That's probably no surprise. But you can test the accuracy of this by noting how many times you yourself gaze at likable objects or persons.

Wouldn't you look often at a new bicycle or family car, a favorite pet, toy, or book? On the other hand, you might not want to see a bad auto accident at all, and would only glance at a person you've been fighting with. A dish of food that is spoiled could make you squint and turn away in disgust.

Recently scientists have discovered other evidence that eye behavior tells without words how we like or dislike something or someone. When the eyes see an object or person that the beholder thinks is pleasant, the pupils enlarge. And a disagreeable sight makes the pupils of the eyes close down.

Such kinds of eye movements cannot be controlled. The pupils react instinctively. But we do determine how we'll look at people when we want to display certain feelings or thoughts.

You've heard of the "cold look," the "come hither look," or a "look of disgust." You've read of eyes that are "knowing," "wise," "twinkling," "steely," or "sad."

Actually, it isn't the eyes that are made to behave in specific ways. Rather, other parts of the face around the eyes are helping to create the silent messages. The nose may be wrinkled and the brows pulled together to show disgust. If eyes look cold or steely it could be because the rest of the face is set and rigid. When the entire face appears relaxed and there is just a small upturn to the mouth, the eyes could look wise or twinkling.

Even eyelids (whether they close briefly or for seconds at a time) can affect meaning, and an eyebrow raised can change an entire facial expression. For example, it is often thought flirtatious to bat one's eyelids. Closing the eyes slowly can be a feminine gesture of superiority or it could say, "Ah, me! The troubles of the world are upon me!"

When a man closes his eyes more than a fraction of a second, the message others read is he's sleepy or bored or disgusted.

Watch the way people raise their eyebrows when you talk. You could decide your story is really surprising them. But let a listener's eyebrows pull down and together, and what then? You could be offending someone or confusing him.

When it comes to conversations, people in this country expect to have on-and-off eye contact while they are talking to each other. The eyes of speaker and listener meet and look away, time and again. In this way, they pick up cues from each other. A speaker sees the listener nod or raise an eyebrow—agreeing or questioning. Or the speaker may discover the listener is not interested in what he has to say. He sees the listener shifting from one foot to the other, or wiggling in a chair, or looking every-which-way. Listeners get signals too. A speaker may glance to the side to say he is not finished speaking or look directly at a listener to say, "Okay, I'm through. It's your turn now."

Young people are often reminded to look at those they are talking to. But behavior studies show that in most conversations, the person talking does not look at the listener as much as the listener looks at the talker.

The speaker (who has the center of attention) drops his gaze before it becomes a stare and makes the listener feel defensive or hostile. If you notice, people who are having an argument seldom drop their gazes. They stare at each other intently. In the same way, people who are fond of each other also keep eye contact. However, other parts of the face and body give added clues as to the differences in feelings—whether people are demonstrating anger or affection, love or hate.

Why is it that some people, whether talking or listening, hardly ever look at others? They drop their eyes, gaze at their feet, or look away from another's face, staring into space or watching things around them. Maybe a person will cover his eyes by rubbing them or put a hand up to a forehead to shield his eyes while talking. What do such gestures tell you?

The person is shy? Trying to hide his feelings? Can't be

trusted? Doesn't like people? Is bored? Disagrees with you? Is tuning you out?

Any of these evaluations could be true. But the downward glance can be a sign of respect, too. In some Spanish-speaking families and some black American families, children are taught that it is defiant to look at a grown-up who is scolding or questioning about some misbehavior. But white middle-class American children are expected to obey an adult's command: "Look at me when I talk to you!"

To a child who learned that eye contact with a grown-up is a signal of *dis*respect, such a command would be impossible to obey, unless the child wanted to signal boldness or to send an "I-don't-care-what-you-do-to-me" message. You can see the problems that would result if a grown-up has learned one meaning for a straightforward glance and a child has learned another!

In order to understand what another person is saying with his actions, it is necessary to at least question whether or not there are differences in the way people have *learned* to act, especially if you are meeting someone for the first time.

Even a very familiar gesture like a smile can be misunderstood. Ask yourself: Does a smile *always* mean that a person is happy or friendly? Could there be smiles that send other messages?

Consider Greg. He's a fifth grader in a northern Indiana elementary school, and he seems to smile constantly. He smiles so much that the gesture gets him into trouble. Recently, the principal of the school called Greg into the office because he'd been teasing girls. As the principal began to scold, Greg started to smile and held his smile even though the principal was getting angrier with every word.

Often a smile on a person's face is a sign of pleasure.

To the principal, Greg's smile seemed like a direct challenge. He thought Greg was being a wise guy and didn't care about his misdeeds. But fortunately the principal soon realized Greg's smile, in this instance, was a way to say, "Hey, I'm sorry" or "Yeah, I did it—I deserve to be chewed out."

Many people smile as a form of apology or as a defensive measure.

A smile can also say, "I'm telling a joke," or can show

that what is being said is not the whole truth. Some people smile to cover up hurts.

From the time you were a few weeks old, you began to learn to smile. And once you entered first grade, you probably had quite a large vocabulary of smiles. By watching facial expressions and by hearing instructions, children learn which kind of smile to use for a particular situation. If you have ever been told to "Wipe that grin off your face!" you know that most grown-ups expect young people to smile only when it's appropriate or proper.

Behavior experts say if children do not learn *how* and *when* to smile "they are isolated for special attention." In other words, if facial expressions don't fit what others expect, you might be labeled disobedient, disrespectful, or even peculiar!

The partial smile on this girl's face is more a silent message for "What is this thing in my hand?" The next expression tells without words that the hot pepper she put in her mouth was not at all to her liking!

THE "EYES" HAVE IT

Some children learn to avoid eye contact, or lower their gaze, as a sign of respect when a grown-up scolds.

When you realize that it's possible to make more than 20,000 different facial expressions (with all variety of positions of the mouth, movement of the eyes and brows, wrinkles of the forehead, and combinations of these), it makes you wonder how anyone ever understands another's look. Fortunately, though, most silent messages of the eyes, face, and head are easily decoded. A look is often supported by spoken words—almost like a caption under a picture—which helps us learn meanings.

And touch may give clues too. Making physical contact with another—touching hands, arms, shoulders, or whatever—is another form of nonverbal speech. But how do you know when to touch and when not to touch? Answering that question is part of understanding body language too.

FOUR
TO TOUCH OR NOT TO TOUCH

If you have ever seen a blind person "look" at someone with his hands, you know how important touch can be in picking up silent messages. By using the fingers to trace the shape and features of the face, a sightless person can get a mental picture of a stranger. This is also a way to view art pieces, such as statues, or to "see" what objects like utensils and tools are like.

The sense of touch helps a blind person determine whether he is with people who are tense or outgoing, sad or happy. The way individuals shake hands, move close to or away from one another, or otherwise make body contact gives clues to personality traits.

Such nonverbal bits of language do not have to be visible to be understood. They are felt or else "seen" in the mind's eye. But touching and being touched are more meaningful when you are fortunate, as most people are, to have the sense of sight. What you see, along with what you touch—AND smell, taste, and hear—provide the total message.

However, with all the sensations you can pick up at the same time, you might get a garbled message once in awhile.

Suppose, for example, you are at a Halloween party. All the lights are out and there are strange, creaking sounds. Eerie whisperings seem to be everywhere. There's the smoky smell of candles snuffed out. People have formed a circle and someone passes around objects to touch—a dish of "eyeballs," a pan of "worms," and a plate of "brains!" Yuk!

Do you believe it? Possibly. Your imagination gets carried away, what with the spooky sounds and the darkness that help support the ghoulish messages you get from touch. When the lights go on again, though, the objects turn out to be peeled grapes, cooked spaghetti, and modeling clay!

The messages of touch don't often fool people, though. From the moment of birth, humans need to be touched. And touching behavior involves more than using the fingers or hands to get the feel of an object or to reach out to another person. It might be holding a baby or linking arms with a friend. It could be shoving with a shoulder or elbowing through a crowd. It might be sitting very close to someone when you are afraid. Or it could be a kiss.

The hands and arms, though, are the parts of the body used for most of the touching gestures. Like the many hand and arm signs that signal important messages, the language of touch is something we are exposed to daily.

Take the simple act of holding a hand. A parent's hand held out is a sign for a child to grasp it, hold it for support—for comfort, for courage, or to steady himself. Holding a grown-up's hand, a child receives a message such as: "Now you are secure; you don't have to be afraid. I'm looking after you."

During the first years of life, humans are often comforted by the sense of touch. Medical and behavior scientists have proven that babies who are *not* held and are seldom touched do not develop as rapidly as those who get Tender Loving Care. Some authorities believe babies even die from the lack of touch or holding. And many infants who seemed hopelessly ill have responded to treatment when body contact was increased. Touching (whether holding, patting, stroking, kiss-

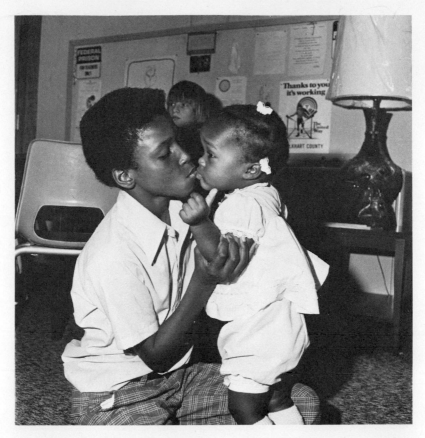

The kiss is one of the most familiar "loving touches," as this boy demonstrates with the baby girl.

ing, hugging, and so on) is as important as food and shelter for healthy growth, because it is a message of love.

In fact, one expert, James J. Thompson, believes that "love is touching." Professor Thompson adds that later on in life "children who are loved by their parents usually do better in school than children who are not." He implies that

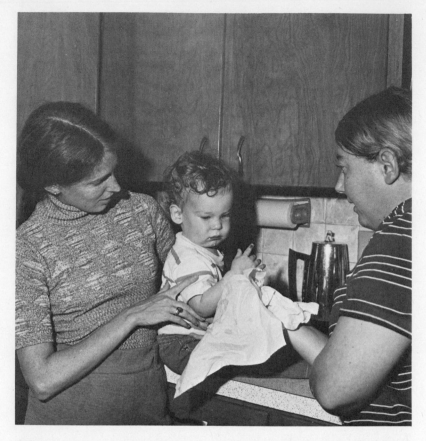

Loving touches also take this form, as a baby is propped on the kitchen sink where mother and friend administer first aid for a cut finger.

children must know or be shown they are loved—through silent messages such as those of touch.

While many studies must yet be made to discover just what "love" is and whether "love is touching," you can do some investigating on your own. See what kinds of messages you get from (and give with) touch.

When you are hurt, ache from an illness, or are insulted, what helps ease the pain or soothe your feelings? A friend's hand on your arm, maybe? Your mother's arm around your shoulders? A supporting pat on the back from your teacher? A quick "pulled-punch" on your upper arm by your older brother? A doctor's firm but gentle grasp? Possibly even a tiny touch by a younger sister tells you someone senses your misery and cares.

The way people use touch to express love or concern depends on the types of people who are touching, and what they have learned from their culture or way of life. Some persons who are shy may only reach out to touch others on rare occasions, while other people almost always use a touch of the hand or a hug to say "I'm with you—I care."

Holding a young child's hand is the kind of touch which silently tells a toddler she's safe or is being protected and cared for.

TO TOUCH OR NOT TO TOUCH

When you investigate the messages of touch, you'll find differences also in the categories of touch. We've started with *Loving Touches*. Now, let's label a few more types.

Greeting Touches could be similar to *Loving Touches*. Close friends and relatives often greet each other (and also show their feelings of affection) by kissing, hugging, and clasping each other's hands. But Greeting Touches are also used by people who meet for the first time and those who don't even like each other. A handshake is a way to say you respect another person. Whether you like him or not, you acknowledge he's part of the human race.

If a person refuses to shake your outstretched hand, you may well be humiliated, feel you've been put down. After an argument or fight it is the handshake which helps opposing parties say: "For the time being, at least, we'll shake/touch and show we are not angry at each other."

A similar touching gesture is used in sports such as wrestling and boxing. Before a bout, the opponents come out of their corners, walk to the center of the ring, and touch hands/gloves to say "Good luck." Afterward, the same touch of boxing gloves and quick embrace says "Good fight" or "The best man won."

Greeting Touches also include such gestures as a man putting a hand to his hat or lifting his hat to say "Hello." Sometimes people "blow kisses"—kiss the hand, extend it out, palm up, and blow across it. These gestures are actually substitutes for touching, when people are too far apart for body contact.

Gestures that substitute for actual contact with another are also used in what you might call approval or *Congratulation Touches*. At sports events, fans sometimes make the "V" sign with the fingers to say they approve a play. This sign indicates the same thing at political rallies or other public events where people want to show they approve of what a speaker says. Of course, the "V" sign is used often to say "Victory!"

Arms raised high over the head with hands clasped show approval, as do two gestures mentioned earlier—the circle made with a thumb and finger, and applause.

When people are able to make body contact, they often kiss, hug, or use a hearty handshake to say "Congratulations!" A slap on the back, a playful punch on the arm, or even a pat on the head can mean the same thing, or say "Good job!"

If you have ever seen a celebrity surrounded by well-wishers, you know how much touch is used to tell the person he or she is admired. There have been many stories about celebrities who have been nearly crushed or injured in some way by those who want to shake hands, grab a sleeve, even tear clothing in an effort to be "in touch" with the famous.

There are also *Teasing and/or Insulting Touches*. These would include such things as using an elbow to poke someone in the ribs. It could be a way to say "This is just a joke." Or the elbowing might demand that someone "Get out of the way!"

If you use both hands to roughly shove someone aside, that kind of touch is not likely to win friends. But if you "steer" someone in a particular direction or gently prod a person with a hand to show where to go, the touch is not offensive.

Teasing with touch is probably used more by boys than by girls. Often boys like to poke, pound, shove, elbow, punch each other. Such touches are not usually meant to injure. Rather, guys use them to show their friendly feelings toward each other. Young girls often show affection by holding hands or putting their arms about each other's waists.

The difference comes from the way of life in this country. A display of love or affection with gentle touches is often considered "feminine behavior." Females have often been categorized as the "weaker sex," while males are supposed to be strong, so behavior that appears to be feminine would be considered by some as a sign of weakness in men or boys. As a result, boys sometimes try to cover up their feelings of affection or display them through rough-and-tumble actions that signify strength.

Fortunately, such ideas about what is a display of strength or weakness or what is masculine or feminine behavior are slowly changing. We have learned, for example, that it is not necessarily a weakness to cry; a strong person can softly caress another. These types of behavior are neither masculine nor feminine—they can be and are used by both sexes. However, it may never become the custom in the United States for men to hold hands, hug, or kiss each other in greeting as is common in some European countries and also in the Middle East.

While poking can often be a way to tease or insult, it has other meanings too. You might put the poking gesture in the category of *Making-a-Point Touches*. Many people emphasize what they are saying by using the index finger to "jab" home a point.

"This is the way it is," a person might say, all the time poking the finger into the listener's arm. If the listener is not used to this type of gesture, the poke could irritate. But in some groups, such a making-a-point gesture is a very natural part of conversation. The amount of this type of touching one does, while talking with another, depends again on background and/or way of life.

You'll notice, though, that there are some fairly common touches that help people get across their ideas when speaking. Some people may be back slappers or arm grabbers. Some might just brush their hands against others' sleeves. Some grasp shoulders, especially when excited.

If people are sitting and talking, a speaker might signal special points in the conversation by tapping the listener on the knee.

Tapping the knee and arm are also gestures that could be called *Togetherness Touches*. These touches often signal that people are expressing the same ideas or are behind the same cause. A business person or politician, for example, might use this kind of touch to show that he and the listener are "on the same wave length" or have been through similar experiences. The conversation itself might be about the weather or the next meeting, but the touches say "We're in this together."

Another Togetherness Touch occurs when a large group of people want to signify unity. At a school pep rally it is not unusual for students to form a circle or line, holding hands while practicing cheers. They link themselves together with touch.

People often touch when they are making introductions. If you say, "This is my friend, Jim," you might reach out to touch Jim on the arm or shoulder. The touch not only shows *who* Jim is, but also that you and he are together.

The most familiar Togetherness Touches are those used by

lovers. A boy and girl in love might let the world know how they feel by holding hands or walking with their arms about each other. A couple might sit face to face with foreheads touching or side by side with one partner resting a head on the shoulder of the other.

Other couples may show they are together by the way they briefly touch each other on the arm or back when they enter a room. They might also brush against each other while talking.

Another category of touching is *Curious Touches*. These are the kind every person uses to learn about the world around him or her. Yet, one of the most common verbal commands a toddler hears is "Don't touch!" And young children are often directed to keep their hands to themselves or told "Hands off!"

Sometimes young hands do cause a lot of mischief and even damage. But there seems to be more emphasis on *non-*touching than on the positive use of touch: To learn. How can you know what a flower is *really* like if you have never touched the petals and stem? What if you could *never* touch any of the things for sale in a store? Would you want to buy them? What would happen if people *always* kept their hands to themselves and never touched each other?

The language of touch is as important a part of the silent body messages as any other. In fact, as described earlier, humans have a common need to be touched. But in modern urban living, people have become isolated from each other. They pull back rather than reach out. They do not want to be involved with one another.

Part of this condition may be due to the fact that, in main-

At play, pushing, shoving, tumbling body touches are part of the silent messages that say "We're having a good time together" or "We're all part of the gang."

stream United States anyway, young people are so often told *not* to touch. They then have trouble understanding when they should. As a result, they are literally "out of touch." They are unable to make contact with people, except on a very impersonal basis.

Grown-ups (in various age groups) have become so alarmed about this impersonal way of life that they are now taking classes or attending sessions in which they are *re*learning how to touch. In many of these groups, people play games which require body contact and learn to touch without embarrassment.

In homes and schools, too, children are learning to be more aware of the sense of touch. Many elementary and secondary students have been through sessions where they have tactile experiences. In other words, they touch objects, plants, animals, and each other. They discover that tactile behavior communicates along with other body movements. It is all part of learning what it is to be *human*.

FIVE
TAKE A STAND

The substitute teacher stalked into the junior high classroom, her thick heels pounding against the tile floor. She faced the class, her body rigid, head tossed back, chin out. She seemed to be trying to stand taller than her five feet three inches as she said: "You have your first assignment. It's on the board. I don't want to hear one sound." Then she ordered crisply: "Open your books and get to work!"

During the entire morning, the substitute teacher held herself "tight" and seemed ready to lash out at the students. She wanted to appear tough. But by mid-morning the students were unimpressed, and a group got together to work out a plan for the kind of behavior the teacher seemed to expect.

Following the noon break, they sat down in their seats and pulled out candy suckers, licking them like little children. This made the substitute teacher so angry she screeched for all those with suckers to throw them away.

Those who didn't were ordered to line up against the wall. The students obeyed. But they turned around, arms over their heads, leaning against the wall as if they were going to be frisked.

Needless to say, the principal was called in and the class was lectured about its misbehavior and disrespect for a teacher.

True, the students used childish actions and postures to show the teacher they didn't think much of her discipline. But what about the substitute? From the minute she entered the classroom, her posture, the way she stood, the way she walked, the way she held herself told the students that she did not trust them. Her body signals (as well as her words) were telling the students that she was on the defensive. By her various postures she was almost daring the kids to "act up." And so they did.

The silent signals of body posture have a lot to do with whether a speaker of any type can gain respect or hold a group's attention. If a speaker, standing in front of a group, shifts his weight from one foot to the other, he might be saying with his posture: "I don't really know where I stand, or what I mean." On the other hand, a speaker who appears at ease, who stands without fidgeting, can make the audience relax—and be attentive.

If someone stuffs his hands in his pockets and drops his head while talking, the silent message coming across could be: "Hmmm, I don't know if I should say this, but. . . ." Or: "I'm going to explain this carefully, one step at a time."

When a person speaks to an individual or group from a sitting position, the *way* he or she sits talks too. Take a business executive or male teacher behind a desk. If he leans back in his chair, clasps his hands behind his head with arms out like wings, the posture looks relaxed. The boss or teacher seems not to care. But he is really putting across the message that he is sure of himself. He is in charge.

Many people in authority use this position to say so. Try the posture and see how it makes you feel. It's a v.i.p. pose!

Sitting, standing, running, walking, skipping, leaning, sauntering—people perform many actions with the body. And whatever one does with his or her body positions can telegraph a message to someone else. This is especially true in sports such as basketball, football, or baseball. Coaches instruct players to look for ways opponents might telegraph what they are going to do.

Anyone who has played or watched these sports knows that members of a team do not want to give away a play that might win points. Thus, players make certain movements to fake a play. A basketball player might lean forward as if to dribble the ball, but whirls and shoots instead. A football player might pretend to pass but this "fake" gives him an opening to run. A runner on base leads off as if to steal home, but only wants to shake up the pitcher.

In sports or everyday living there are many different messages sent with positions of the body. But how do you figure out what a person says with posture?

As with other types of visible behavior, posture cannot be taken out of context. You have to see the whole picture in order to understand the total message. But here are a few broad examples of how postures express states of mind and health, emotions, and even a person's rank or status in a group.

Imagine your father in his workshop. He is looking at parts for the lawn mower which are strewn across the workbench. He stands with his feet spread apart, his body leaning slightly forward, head down, rubbing the back of his neck with one hand. From that posture (and clues from the rest of the scene) what would you conclude as you walked in? Well, it's *not* the time to ask pop for a raise in your allowance!

Check out another scene. Young people are packed into an auditorium to watch a show. A magician is on stage, performing a variety of tricks. He seems to be pulling rabbits,

In training, a young boxing student has to learn how to defend himself. Body stances, positions of the hands and arms, and body movements are extremely important to protect oneself from the other guy's punches in the ring.

cards, scarves, and all manner of objects from everywhere imaginable. The show is a great success—as just about anyone can tell from postures of people in the audience. Some sit, leaning partially forward, watching intently. Others are upright in their seats, almost at attention. And some might appear in more relaxed or reclining positions, but their heads are jutting forward.

Posture can tell you a great deal about a person's attitude. Usually people tense their bodies when they are listening or watching with interest. That doesn't mean being uptight or rigid. Rather, people hold a position of "forwardness" or "openness." They seem to be taking in what is going on around them. Just the opposite is true in a situation like this one:

A salesman is talking to a group. The men slouch in their chairs. The women lean their heads on their hands with elbows propped on the table. A few have their arms crossed. But most are so overrelaxed they look like wet noodles draped over furniture. The message? No sale! The group let the salesman know they were not interested—they were bored—and wouldn't buy.

Here's another scene: An older sister is working a crossword puzzle. Her posture should tell you whether or not she wants to be disturbed. She might be hunched over at a table, staring at the squares and lists of words. The tip of her pencil is in her mouth or else her tongue might protrude slightly between her teeth. Such body positions often signal concentration. A person in such a posture is usually in deep thought and does not want to be bothered.

When looking for clues as to what body posture has to tell you, there's no better place to observe than at a busy airport or train station. People may exhibit impatience by the way they pace back and forth. A person who is not too uptight about waiting may sit casually on a seat or lean easily against a post, watching the parade of people go by. Then there are "expectant" postures, as people press against railings, lean forward, watching for relatives or friends who are arriving. There are slumped postures that indicate disappointment or sadness. Postures can also say a person is eager to visit a new place or is confused or tired of traveling.

Boredom, excitement, happiness, sorrow, and many other human conditions are shown with posture. You already know about one posture that demonstrates confidence: sitting with hands clasped behind the head. Other postures also say "I'm in charge." A store manager or floor walker might pace with his shoulders "squared," head tilted back, eyes watchful. He's letting people know by the way he carries himself that he has authority.

Young guys on the street show their "cool" (or self-confidence) and manhood by standing in a group with arms folded high on their chests, muscles tensed, chins forward, heads back. Then there's the army sergeant's posture. His hands are placed behind his back, chest thrust out, in an "at-attention" position that leaves no doubt who has the final word!

A policeman's stance is another familiar pose. He "anchors" himself with feet spread slightly apart. His thumbs

This posture is often used to show dominance or that a person is in charge of a situation.

may be caught in his belt; chest and chin are thrust forward. He says with his posture, "I am here to enforce the law." In contrast, one body language expert, Dr. Scheflen, shows that a policeman in another country would not use such posture. The Italian cop, for example, would be more likely to lean forward when talking to a person, rubbing his hands together. He would be showing that he is a "servant of the people."

Now, picture this: A man is rushing to a hospital emergency room with his wife who is going to deliver a baby. He races across town, through stop signs and red lights. At the hospital the man does not immediately recog-

TAKE A STAND

nize the doctor in charge. He talks to a woman in a white coat, but all the time looks past her. His posture seems to say, "I'm ready to run; why are you in my way?"

But suddenly the man realizes he is talking to the emergency room doctor. The woman in the white coat is a physician and will take care of the expectant mother until her own doctor comes.

How did the father-to-be figure this out? Not from words alone, since he was in no state to really listen to what was being said.

The doctor's posture, a female version of "squaring off," helped get the message across. The doctor held herself tall and let the man see she was able to handle the situation.

The type of nervousness shown by the father-to-be is often a subject for drama. And actors on stage, TV, or in the movies depend a great deal on posture to send messages to their audiences. If a character is supposed to be in a state such as that of the expectant father, the actor plays the role with many postures and gestures. He might pace quickly across the stage, with shoulders hunched, or huddle in a chair, clasping his hands tightly together.

Suppose an actor wanted to portray a drunk. This would have to be shown with posture as well as slurred speech. How would the actor sit or stand? Certainly not like the sergeant or the store manager or the doctor. Try out various postures in front of a mirror. You'll soon see (and feel) how positions of the body almost shout a message.

Do you want to show fear? The body seems to get rigid, tensing for flight. There's a surprise waiting? Watch the body change and appear more relaxed, but still ready for action. Are you going to show scorn or superiority? Your head automatically snaps back so you can "look down your nose!"

Actors and actresses often practice postures and gestures of this type. These are important techniques to master for the theater.

We play many roles as we progress through life and often learn to fib effectively with our posture and body positions. For example, in school students soon discover there are times when they should look busy with an assignment or act innocent even though they may not be.

The point is, for survival and to get along with others, it is often necessary to assume postures that fit particular situations. In a church or temple, you would not expect to see anyone lying on the floor—unless of course this is part of a religious ceremony, such as in the Muslim faith. If you saw a large group of people sitting on a curb at State and Madison (one of the world's busiest corners) in Chicago, wouldn't you be surprised? Such postures don't fit big city ways. Or how about standing like a soldier all during a ball game? It doesn't make sense, except when the posture goes along with a flag ceremony or similar event.

The rules for what to do in a particular situation are not as strict as they used to be. Women, for instance, do not have to sit primly with legs pressed together, feet flat on the floor. The pants suits and other new clothing styles and attitudes have helped to change that. And children in school do not always stand to recite as was once the case.

However, no matter where you are—on a bus, at a job, in a store, at a park—there are certain behaviors expected of people. Postures may reflect the individual somewhat but they also conform or go along with what the majority is doing. An unusual body posture sends a message to observers that the person is "way out."

In noting postures, there's this to remember: The body can

It's clear from the facial expressions and body positions that the two young people are "into" the sounds as they dance to the music coming from the record player.

assume nearly a thousand different positions, but people usually use only a few common ones. While growing up, each person learns patterns for posing and holding his or her body, just as we all learn gestures, facial expressions, and the language of touch. These patterns add to the vocabulary, or coded symbols, of body talk.

SIX
DON'T BURST THE BUBBLE

There are lots of ways to say "That's mine!" Put a sweater or jacket over a seat next to you at a ball game. The seat is marked as yours—saved or held for someone you know. Or else it indicates that you'd like space between you and the next person.

While you look through the card catalog at the library, put a book on a table. You say the spot belongs to you.

Spread a blanket on the beach. You lay out a boundary that marks a section of sand as yours. It includes not only the blanket area, but also several feet around it.

Sit in the middle of a park bench and you say, "I've claimed this bench—it's mine for awhile." But slide off center a bit, and you say you are willing to share the space.

All of this is to point out *territory*. Behavior experts know each person stakes out an area or space to call his own. Even young children—at home, in school, on the playground— find ways to mark places as theirs. Thus, space is related to body language. It says without words what is your "turf," or territory. Space also tells something about your attitude toward others.

From the study of how animals, birds, and fish mark their own and sense others' territories, scientists have been able to determine some ways man uses space. They know humans *need* territory, or places of their own.

Dr. Edward T. Hall, an anthropologist, was one of the first scientists to study the way "space speaks." He believes that

Sometimes people use space to show that they want to be alone, as this young boy does on the playground, isolating himself from the others.

each human being, like other animals, has various zones in which to move about or just to be in. Dr. Hall discovered that every person has an invisible "bubble" around him. This bubble is really a person's own private space or territory. And it is a way to describe the distance we all want to keep between ourselves and other people or things.

The poet W. H. Auden described it this way: "Some thirty inches from my nose, the frontier of my Person goes, . . . Beware of rudely crossing it: I have no gun, but I can spit."

You might also think in terms of invisible antennae, or "feelers." Humans seem to be equipped with some type of receivers that pick up messages telling when their space has been invaded. No one wants another person to move in on his or her own space, unless permission has been granted.

Maybe you are not aware that you have a private space, or bubble, surrounding you. But it's easy to understand that a certain *place* is yours—a seat at a table or a spot on a beach. You learn about such territories at home. Maybe you have your own bed, and even your own room. There's a place at home for your toys, books, and other personal belongings. For that matter, each member of your family probably has certain places in the home to call his or her own.

When it comes to the invisible bubble around each person, that is a little different. Most people do not share their bubble space with others unless they are part of a family or are fond of one another. People tend to put distance (or space) between those things and persons they do not know or dislike.

There are several kinds of distances people maintain. Dr. Hall labels them *intimate, personal, social,* and *public.* Intimate distance is of course being very close to another, as in a family. Personal distance might be the kind people put between themselves at a party. Social distance is more businesslike and formal. People stay anywhere from four to twelve feet apart. Public distance is used by actors, politicians, and leaders before a large group.

There has been much study and more will be done in how people use these different distances. Dr. Hall has called this

Here, the young boy pulls away from a grown-up and a little girl who are trying to engage him in conversation. This is a common reaction when a person's private space has been invaded, even though a person might not be aware that others are moving in on his or her territory.

study the science of *proxemics* (from the word *proximity*, meaning "nearness"). Simply put, proxemics is the study of how people use space to relate to each other and things around them. Scientists determine why, when, and where people allow nearness or use space as a barrier to protect themselves from others.

Since proxemics (like kinesics) is a new science, there are few definite conclusions about the meaning of spaces separating people. But you can make some very general observations of your own. Take note of how you use space on different occasions. What messages do you get from other people as they move close to or away from you? Does distance give you a feeling that you are being ignored? When do you feel crowded?

Standing in line at a store counter or to buy tickets, you can learn about space. People keep just enough distance between each other so that their bubbles are intact. If you should move in on another's bubble area, you would soon know it. That person would fidget or turn around to show you the irritation on his face. Or a person who feels crowded might ask you to "get back" or even shove you aside.

In school, you often hear teachers tell students not to crowd in line. And it's not unusual for fights to erupt if someone is shoved or pressed too close.

School is a good place to study the use of space and how people mark territory. You usually have a desk or part of a table to call your own. How do you feel when you find someone sitting at your desk? How do you react if someone clutters your place at a table with papers and books? Chances are, you become defensive. You want to protect your area. First you claim your spot by saying it belongs to you. Then you might move others' belongings aside. You might even ask people to leave.

Watch, too, how people arrange themselves when seats are *not* assigned. In a classroom, some students will always pick back row seats. Others will always sit near the front of the room or along the sides. Generally, the students who do not

DON'T BURST THE BUBBLE

The two girls have marked off their own space at the table, as have the two boys in the background. The bodies facing each other, and the objects (such as the puzzle the girls are putting together), also help mark territory.

want to take part in activities will put distance between themselves and the teacher. Those who like to be involved choose seats closer to the teacher.

Other classroom behavior gives clues about what space says. A student who is a leader often takes a "head" position at a table. You might note that students who work well together usually sit side-by-side. Students who do not like a teacher seldom go near him or her. They keep their distance. But they attempt to sit or stand close by a teacher who is liked. When students often gather around a teacher, this is usually a sign that the teacher is very well liked or a favorite in the school.

However, even a favorite teacher is not welcome in a student's bubble area. If a teacher stands very close to a student's desk, the teacher is not respecting the student's private space. Without realizing it, the teacher is saying the student is a nonperson. And naturally that brings about reactions. The student might start swinging a leg or tapping a pencil on his desk. His actions occur without thought and say that he feels crowded. The student is signaling for the teacher to move back.

What happens to space on the playground? The first thing you would notice is that students form groups, some "closed" and some "open." Take a group of cheerleaders. They are planning a routine for the next game. They stand in a circle, facing each other. If you approached the group, you would feel unwelcome. The circle would not break. Bodies would be close together and you would have to look at the cheerleaders' backs. The group is definitely a closed one. No one else can be a part of it, at least for that moment.

An open group might not be as easy to spot. Two people could be standing or sitting close together. But they are facing away from each other just slightly. A foot or arm might be pointing out, away from the two. There would be space left for another person to join them.

On the playground you often see one person standing as if

DON'T BURST THE BUBBLE

on an island. He or she is surrounded by a lot of space. Sometimes that person wants privacy and uses distance from others to say so. Or the boy or girl might be shy. Distance can indicate loneliness or fear.

Did you know people sometimes use space, like posture, to dominate or control others? When questioning prisoners, police invade private space. They move in on prisoners, stand over them, or sit almost touching them to frighten and subdue. Invasion of space is a method for obtaining confessions.

Parents or teachers may get very close or bend over children when scolding. This too destroys private space. It makes a child feel smaller, insecure, unable to fight back.

A boss might stand right next to an employee to inspect his work. This closeness makes the worker feel unsure. He might think the boss is threatening him.

You've probably seen the baseball manager who stands nose-to-nose with an umpire. He is challenging the umpire's call. By moving in on the umpire's bubble, the baseball manager hopes the umpire will "back down." But the umpire is used to such invasion of territory. He "stands his ground" and does not change his call. The player is out!

If someone moves in on your private territory, you probably sense it immediately. But what about the other guy? Not all people have the same size bubbles. There are differences in the amount of private space people need.

Many people from Mexico, Puerto Rico, and some South American countries do not have as large private bubbles as people in mainstream United States. This is true also of black, Jewish, Indian, Arab, Italian, Oriental, and other cultural groups where closeness is allowed. People stand or sit within touching distance while speaking to each other. So anyone who backs off to protect his larger private bubble would seem like a snob—"standoffish"—to a person who knows only close spacing. By the same token, a person who needs "thirty inches from his nose" for private space would feel "pushed" by close contact.

Whether close together or far apart, you can see that space does indeed "speak." The meaning of space vocabulary, though, depends on many factors, among them individual differences and cultural patterns. What is most important in space dialogue is whether people respect each other's bubbles. Bursting another's bubble might be okay when blowing soap suds, but not when a person's own special territory is invaded. That kind of bubble-bursting could be body language for "War!"

SEVEN

STOP, LOOK, AND LISTEN

With all the emphasis on visible behavior, it isn't news that it takes eyes as well as ears to "hear" another person's message. When someone speaks to you, he or she usually uses both verbal and nonverbal ways to communicate. As you listen, you look for body language and facial expressions that go along with the spoken words. At the same time, you can also be tuning in on the *way* people speak.

Is the voice quavering? Does the person sound worried when talking? What happens to the voice as the person tells an exciting story? Do some people growl when they're angry?

Whatever the tone of voice it is usually reinforced with some type of body language. When someone wants to communicate friendliness, for instance, the voice tone is probably light and easy—it might even have a bit of a rhythm or ring to it. Facial expressions would be relaxed. Gestures could be open or reaching out. The body might be somewhat tense with interest.

An emotion like sadness might be communicated with low voice tones and hardly any variation in the pitch, plus an unsmiling face and drooping body posture.

You can probably mimic many different examples of voice patterns and tell how these reflect a mood, emotion, or attitude. These variations are seldom taught formally. Instead, meanings of voice tones, like body language messages, are learned from infancy, through experience, hearing and seeing clusters of behavior time and time again.

Even so, much more can be learned through good listening. In fact, experts have determined that most people only listen at about 25 percent efficiency. That means, about three-fourths of the sounds and words people *actually hear* "go in one ear and out the other," as the old saying puts it. The meanings of most sounds do not register.

To increase understanding of others' messages, it seems to follow that one should be a good listener. But it's not easy. It takes patience, skill, and quite a bit of effort to listen effectively. And sometimes one has to ignore body language in order to tune in on the verbal message. Certain gestures, postures, and so on can jam the air waves because they attract more attention than the spoken words.

Body language most often gets in the way of verbal messages when a speaker has peculiar mannerisms, doesn't behave as expected, or wears an unusual outfit. Here's an exaggerated example. Suppose a teacher came into the room wearing a long stringy gray wig and a pointed hat, carrying a broom, hunched over, and shaking a finger as she talked in a "crackling" voice. Would you really hear her if she proceeded to discuss the lessons as usual?

Of course such a situation would be highly improbable. But there can be some very common behaviors that affect one's ability to listen. A continual tap of the foot, a lopsided smile, a cough, a shrill voice, a deep frown, and countless other actions can distract. The trick is to concentrate on the spoken words and not think about behavior that annoys or competes for attention.

Another barrier to good listening is faking attention. Students learn early how to sit as if listening to a teacher while off in their own dream world. And many grown-ups pretend to listen to children by nodding and murmuring "mmhmm," but all the while they are busily engaged in some activity such as looking at a newspaper, cooking, washing the car, and so on. Sometimes faking attention becomes a habit. A person can get used to not listening and won't make any effort to tune in. As mentioned in previous chapters, if a person is truly interested in what a speaker has to say, the body will be somewhat tense. The listener will have off-and-on eye contact with the speaker or, if at a distance, at least be watching for added clues to the speaker's ideas that come across in body language.

Some people "close their minds" when listening—which means they don't really listen at all. Instead, they spend all the time while a person is speaking to make up their own arguments or to think about how much they dislike the speaker. A person can also turn off on subjects that seem dull or very complex. And poor health or some physical condition like hunger or a painful injury can block off the messages of speech.

To repeat, being a good listener is no simple task. It's hard work to stay tuned in and develop skills of concentration.

You can practice at home by eliminating distractions such as record playing and TV while someone speaks. With friends or in a classroom try not to interrupt a person who's talking. Let a person finish what he or she has to say before you begin. When you have to listen to long speeches or instructions, try to pick out the points that will be helpful to you.

Even while speaking you can be a good listener. Here

When listening to another person talk, some people close themselves off, or tune out, such as this girl could be doing. She folds her arms across herself and seems to be saying with her body language that she has no interest in the "show-off" behavior and talk of the boy on the left.

again, knowing body language helps. You can get "feedback"—the gestures, facial expressions, posture of a listener tell you how your words are being accepted. Somebody covers a yawn, another person fiddles with things on a table, a third person fidgets in a chair as you speak. The message

STOP, LOOK, AND LISTEN

from listeners could be: "We're bored." As the speaker you would be smart to act on the feedback by changing your speaking style, shifting to some other topic, or even asking someone else to speak.

Sales people, negotiators (those who help opposing parties reach agreements), people in helping professions such as counselors and social workers, often make use of feedback. It is part of a control mechanism. In other words, if a speaker notices the feedback of his listeners, he can try to change any unfavorable reaction to his words. The cues come from what a person does while listening.

Listening behavior is another part of the communication process. Someone can be sending you a silent message while you are speaking or you can be sending one yourself as you listen. The verbal and nonverbal go back and forth at the same time.

EIGHT
THE BIG COVER-UP

Recently a bank in the midwest advertised that it was giving away dollar bills. But there was a catch. Customers could only collect if a bank employee waited on them *without* a smile. The purpose was to show the public that the bank was a pleasant place to do business. And bank officials bet on success. Each employee was expected to greet customers with a smile—or else pay out the dollar bill!

Why all the emphasis on the smile? What if an employee was disgusted, unhappy, or irritated? Why cover up if you don't like something or someone?

To answer that, think how you would react if you walked into a store to buy a sweater and a clerk scowled, pointed to the back, and mumbled: "Look on the corner table." Right away you would have doubts about staying. Then, suppose the clerk followed you around with a hand on a hip, looking you up and down, lips pressed together. You would quickly feel uncomfortable. Who would want to buy anything from an old grouch like that? Out the door you would go—fast!

Most sales and business people know the importance of presenting a pleasant front to the public. This attracts customers and increases sales. In fact, many sales persons, especially those who go into homes or call on buyers in their offices, take classes in how to use body language to help convince customers they should buy. For example, a salesman could learn how to show he is trustworthy. He might sit on the edge of his chair, lean forward, arms out, and gesture with his hands open, palms showing. If he is wearing a suit coat, he'll have it unbuttoned; this is a sign of openness. No doubt he will be smiling. These actions could say to the customer that the salesman is open and friendly, and therefore must be honest—a person to do business with.

Many politicians also practice open gestures in order to appear sincere. They might reach out to clasp a hand on a person's shoulder or raise their arms in broad, outward gestures while speaking. Sometimes a politician puts on a ''poker face'' (with no expression) when he does not want others to know his views on a controversial subject.

People wear ''masks'' and use body language cover-ups for a variety of purposes. Some help or protect others. Doctors, for example, learn to control their facial expressions so that patients cannot read negative reactions to illnesses or injuries. If a doctor shows concern or worry, this would alarm most patients and might make their physical conditions worse.

Lawyers, counselors, and other professionals who work with people on a personal basis have to show interest in their clients' problems. Maybe a lawyer has had a sleepless night or is anxiously waiting for an important phone call. This must be covered up. The lawyer sits quietly in a ''thinker position'' or takes notes while the client talks. Such actions tell the client, ''What you think, feel, and say are the only important things now.'' And that might be all the client

It looks as though the girl on the rope swing is eager to take her turn. But the smile on her face covers up her real feelings— apprehension or fear. Her expression changes, revealing her true feelings, as she's up, up, and away!

wants—someone to listen while he or she talks.

Grown-ups sometimes disguise their fears so their children will not learn them. Maybe a mother is afraid of deep water, but she'll try not to show this when she teaches her two-year-old how to jump into her arms while in a swimming pool. Or she might be afraid of storms. Yet the mother will smile and go about her usual routine in a relaxed way while thunder and lightning rage outside. She'll use body language to show she's calm, hoping this will also be picked up by her family.

In school, a teacher might cover up certain feelings or attitudes to keep order. What if the fire bell goes off? Immediately most students would begin to file out of classrooms as they've learned to do in the practice drills. But suddenly someone discovers there's smoke in the halls. Another sees flames coming from the cafeteria. The students might begin to push, shove, stumble, and try to run over each other to get out. But the teacher must move everyone along as in the practice drill, gesturing and directing students to stay in line, thus leading the way to safety. Order has to be maintained (no matter what the teacher's personal fears) to prevent injuries and even death.

The need for order brings about a variety of different cover-ups. Think about how people act in crowded public places. Even if a person feels irritable or unhappy, he uses the smile to keep others from reacting angrily. When there's jostling, such body contact could be considered a threat or an invasion of private space. So individuals smile as a way to apologize for bumping into others.

In a restaurant, a quick way to get attention would be to shout or whistle at a waiter. But most people raise a hand or jerk the head back slightly to bring the waiter to the table. The silent message is understood and preserves a peaceful and quiet atmosphere in the dining room.

At some business parties, quite a few people might use cover-ups for a variety of reasons. Maybe the host is the owner of a large manufacturing company. Guests are executives and sales people for the firm, buyers who order large quantities of goods from the company, and potential buyers—those who might do business with the company at some later date. At such parties, there are usually some guests who prefer to be somewhere else, but they still "put on a happy face." For example, a salesman might dislike a potential buyer but he laughs and jokes with him. Another employee of the company might be bored with the party but he wears a happy mask whenever he goes near the boss. In the first instance, the salesman could be using a cover-up to help increase business and earn extra pay for himself. In the second, the employee might be hoping to get a job promotion.

People also use body language cover-ups in embarrassing and humorous situations. Have you ever seen a grown-up trip over a small crack in the sidewalk? Did he or she then look around to see if anyone had been watching? The grown-up would not want to appear silly or clumsy, so with body language cover-ups a different message would be sent out. The grown-up might scowl at the sidewalk or even stop to stare at the crack, as if to tell onlookers: *"Anyone* could trip over that obstacle!"

Maybe you know someone who always brags about the kinds of tricks he or she can do. What if such a person tries to show you a special trick with a yo-yo or some clever twists

THE BIG COVER-UP

and turns with the jump rope—and then gets all tangled up in the string or rope? You might be on the verge of laughter, but suddenly notice that the other person is sending out silent messages of anger, with a frown, tight lips, and so on. What would you do then? You might swallow your laughter, hide your smile behind your hand, and turn away. Even though the entanglement is funny, you might decide to cover up rather than risk an argument or fight with the other person, who is not really upset with you. The anger is merely another type of cover-up; the person does not want to let on that he or she is embarrassed because of a trick-gone-wrong.

Another way people cover up mistakes or small failures is to swagger or use some posture that shows triumph. Such a cover-up can help protect a person from ridicule. A strut or proud body position can say: "Don't you *dare* laugh at me and destroy my dignity or I'll be angry."

On the other hand, there are people who use the strut or swagger to impress others with their importance. They might feel like nobodies or think they do not rank high with others. They want to have status. So they send messages which are supposed to express superiority with gestures, facial expressions, and distance from others. Even the clothes, homes, and cars such people own can become nonverbal ways to say: "I'm above everyone else and can't be bothered with those who don't have as much as I do."

Those who are discriminated against might try to make up for this with "show-off" behavior too. For example, some black men on the street lounge against cars or buildings in overrelaxed poses or stand with heads back and chests expanded. Either way, the body language says, "We don't care what others think—we'll do our own thing."

Just about every school or neighborhood has a "bully"—someone who uses aggressive body language to hide the fact that he feels like a nobody. He might shove a little person around. Or pick a fight with anyone he knows he can beat. Or constantly swagger and talk like a tough guy. This disguise might work until someone comes along who won't accept the bully's actions and will win out in a fight!

Even so, bully behavior can be a necessary cover-up in neighborhoods where only toughness is respected. In other words, a person might have to act unafraid and able to defend himself in order to prevent others from attacking him.

Another type of cover-up is used on jobs and in schools by those who don't want to work or study. People act busy in order to avoid real effort.

Jamie is such a person. During study periods in junior high school, he seldom talks or bothers others. He keeps to himself and always seems to be involved with his books and papers. He often goes to the pencil sharpener and grinds away on his pencil. He looks at books on a shelf, frowning and biting his lower lip as if in a deep study. When at his desk or table, he shuffles his papers about and keeps a book open in front of him. Sometimes he scratches his head and cocks it to one side. These and many other gestures are designed to fool others. Such behavior can send a nonverbal message: "Look. I'm studious and industrious." A person in authority such as a teacher (or a boss on the job) would conclude that real work is being done. The person is producing.

Of course when results are measured, in tests of learning or in goods and services produced, the game is up. The cover-up will no longer be effective.

Just a few of the different situations in which people put on disguises have been mentioned. Body language cover-ups are used to improve business, to get along with others and keep order, to impress, and also to help a person feel good about himself. Even in churches, temples, or other religious places, where people might be expected to search themselves for wrongdoing, the masks of the do-gooder might be worn. People want an acceptable self-image—that is, almost everyone wants to see himself as a proper person, someone of value.

As you begin to notice the types of cover-ups people use, you will probably wonder if anyone ever goes through life being just himself. The fact is, each person has many sides to his or her personality. No one acts the same for every encounter or meeting with others. The way people interact (how one behaves in relation to another person) depends on what each has learned about others, the personalities involved, their physical makeup, the place, and even such conditions as the time and weather.

More and more, behavior experts are emphasizing the need to drop disguises that have developed over many years. Some people cover up too much, wear masks for most of each day. Then it becomes difficult for them to relax and ''be for real.''

As psychiatrists explain it, people sometimes poison themselves by holding back their honest feelings and attitudes. Facial masks and fake body language are used because people are afraid of their own feelings and of others' reactions. They cannot express anger, joy, hate, love, excitement, and a whole range of other emotions and conditions. Quite often mental and physical illnesses develop.

It's true that we have to play different roles in different situations. We cannot give vent to honest emotions twenty-four hours a day or be literally truthful each time we communicate. Chaos would result. Some cover-ups aid survival just as some animal or insect colors act as camouflages to protect against attack. But one has to find times and places to express what he or she truly is. Otherwise, one is a puppet, a robot, a thing in a shell. And who wouldn't rather be a human being with a variety of emotions and attitudes that make up his or her individual personality?

NINE
READING OTHERS

The more aware you become of body movements and positions, the more you will try to decode the silent messages of people around you. Perhaps you'd like to know whether another person is a friendly, happy individual and easy to get along with. Could you read this from body language? Sure, if you look for clusters of gestures and behavior that *generally* show openness and cooperation. You would watch for expressions and body movements that signal expansion or reaching out.

One member of a group waves at you and motions for you to join them. A person smiles and taps you on the arm. Someone clasps you around the shoulders and nods several times. These can all be signals that help you identify friendly people.

The same type of open or outgoing body language often expresses happiness. This is one of the basic human emotions that you will be able to read from silent messages. Usually it's easy to recognize in relaxed body movements and full smiles. The opposite emotion, sadness or depression, is easy to read too. You would be on the lookout for drooping postures, a slowdown of gestures, and few changes in facial expressions.

Surprise and fear are other basic emotions that you can spot quickly. Both are often reflected in the face, with wide open eyes and mouth. Yet, there are slight differences in these facial expressions. You would read "surprise" if a per-

It wouldn't be difficult to "read" the expression on this little girl's face. You can tell with a glance that she's concentrating on the art work on her desk.

son's mouth opened in a full smile and there was a general "upturn" of facial wrinkles. If a person's facial features become almost fixed and the mouth sags open, then you could probably assume that person is afraid. Sometimes a hand or fist goes quickly to the mouth or over the heart in fear or in horror. That can happen in surprise too. However, once again there is a difference. A person who is surprised probably would not pull back or "pull in on himself/herself" as much as a fearful person would.

Another basic emotion that you often read in others is

READING OTHERS

anger or irritation. It seems you could identify the visible behavior for that emotion with no trouble at all. There are often explosions—yelling, scolding, pounding or kicking objects, fighting, and so on. Before that point, though, people vent their steam in a variety of ways.

Beginning anger often appears as a "tight smile"—the lips curve but the rest of the face does not relax. Or the lips might be set rigidly in a straight line.

People become tense and tight when they are getting angry. You can almost see a wall or barrier being set up, as if a rigid body will prevent any more hurts from getting through. There is little need, at such times, for a person to say, "I'm mad at the world and turned off." The condition is obvious.

As with other emotions, no two people would show irritation and the build-up of anger just exactly alike. But you soon discover that there are clusters of body language commonly used for that particular emotion.

When irritated, people often say such things as "He's a pain in the neck" or "She gets in my hair." Gestures sometimes support the words, or gestures are used in place of the common sayings. A person shows the "pain" by rubbing the back of the neck and tries to scratch or brush aside the "irritation" of the hair.

You've seen ball players who get angry at other team members or upset with themselves when they make mistakes in a game. One might pull off a hat or helmet, then vigorously scratch at his head or kick at the ground. He might rub the back of his neck with his head bowed, while the features of his face pull together in a scowl. A player might even throw a helmet or slam a bat to the ground.

In anger, a person often "bares" his teeth; the facial expression is similar to a smile, but you know that this is not a silent message for friendliness.

A person's anger or frustration with ideas can be shown with clenched hands on a table or in the lap. Some men use "hot-under-the-collar" gestures. Watch a man run a finger under his collar, purse his lips, and jut his chin out. It's likely that he's working up to anger.

There are many human conditions that border on the basic

READING OTHERS

emotions just described. Nervousness and defensive attitudes, for example, are often expressed with body language similar to that used for anger. Rigidness, neck rubbing, clenched fists can indicate a person is "on guard."

Take a young girl, Karen, who is worried about speaking in front of her class. She sits rigidly at her desk, lips tight, her hands clenched together. If someone approaches her, she might turn away and become even more rigid, or she might stalk out of the room. The body language could read: "I'm angry or irritated—down on everyone." However, you have to take in the total situation. If you know Karen is shy and seldom talks to others, her actions read differently. They are her way of defending herself from her fears of the group.

People use a variety of defensive gestures to protect themselves from pressures, stress, hurt feelings, and so on. You know a few of them if you have ever folded your arms across your chest when someone brings up an unpleasant subject in conversation. You also use a defensive gesture when you back away from a grown-up who seems to be smothering you by closing in on your bubble area or private space. You could raise a hand to your mouth in a defensive gesture if you are not sure of what you want to say or feel self-conscious talking to someone.

Confusion, bewilderment, boredom, doubt, disgust, contempt, determination are other common human conditions that can be read in others if you look for the right clues. A furrowed brow and fidgeting might be a sign of confusion. Boredom is commonly shown by tapping a foot or fingers, or by crossing one's legs and swinging a foot toward an exit.

Doubt is not an easy attitude or condition to identify. But it is apparent in a photo of President Nixon and Senator

Edward Kennedy that was published in a picture story for *Life Magazine* several years ago. The photo shows the President talking with Senator Kennedy. He seems to be trying to convince or "sell" the Senator on an idea or project. The Senator's head is bowed slightly, his forehead furrowed and eyebrows arched. He is scratching his neck with his right hand. Whatever the President's proposal, Senator Kennedy's gestures clearly state: "I'm not convinced, Mr. President—I don't buy your idea."

If you have ever known anyone you think is "snooty" or "uppity" you have probably gotten this impression from body language that expresses disgust or contempt. A person often fits the description with the nose (or snoot) pushed high in the air, maybe even a quick sniff accompanying the gesture. The head is thrown back in an *up*pity position. All of this is done to say, "I'm above most people and find those beneath me not worth dealing with."

An attitude of determination might not come through in the silent messages of body language as much as in forceful words. It's difficult to identify this human state. But you can see some examples of determination gestures when the well-known evangelist, Billy Graham, appears on television. Turn off the sound and you'll notice right away that Preacher Graham uses an index finger constantly. Over and over again he points to make a point. The finger jabs the air, pounds the Bible, pokes at the audience. His fist too is often used to pound home a point. Or his hand cuts through the air like a karate chop. You know the preacher is determined to get his message to his audience.

No matter how often you read common gesture clusters and correctly identify human conditions or emotions, there

You saw these two young people dancing in a previous picture. But now there are others in the scene. What do you read from their body language? Is the boy in the forefront bored with the whole thing or tired or embarrassed by his older brother's antics? Is the little girl with folded arms mocking grown-up behavior to show "interest" in the total scene? Or is this just her way to show she is not quite "with" the older generation?

will be times when you will misunderstand body language. You might judge a cluster of gestures or body movements too quickly. Or your own negative feelings on a particular day could affect your interpretation of silent messages.

Carla had that experience. She had just moved into a new neighborhood and had to go to a new school down the block.

There were twin girls, Pat and Pam, who lived next door. Carla wanted to ask the twins to walk to school with her. But the first time Carla waved at the twins outside their home they started to whisper to each other. As Carla moved cautiously along the walk toward the twins, she saw them smiling and heard one of them say: "That's the new girl from the East. She'll have. . . ."

Carla didn't hear the rest. Immediately, she whirled and ran across the street. Because the twins were talking about her and did not wave back, Carla had decided at once that the girls disliked her and were laughing at her. She walked on to school alone, her head up, looking straight ahead. She avoided the twins for weeks.

It wasn't until the girls went shopping with their mothers in the neighborhood supermarket that they were forced to meet. Carla and her mother practically collided with the twins and their mother as they pushed carts through the aisle. The mothers recognized each other as neighbors and introduced themselves and their daughters. Carla could no longer avoid the twins. They all had to speak and soon discovered they had been misreading each other. They began chatting away like old friends.

The twins explained that on that first day of school, they had been telling each other how cute they thought Carla was. They were going to tease her about all the boys that would swarm around a new and pretty girl. It really surprised them when Carla stalked off, without speaking or even glancing at them. The twins decided Carla's good looks must have made her "stuck up."

No doubt you can recall instances when you, too, put the wrong meanings to gestures and facial expressions. All

READING OTHERS

through life these types of misunderstandings go on. Maybe you have even formed stereotypes. For example, if you decide that all pretty girls are "stuck up" just because one pretty girl (like Carla) *seemed* to be, then you have formed a stereotype. You have concluded that all in one group are just like one person who represents that group.

It's not easy to prevent forming stereotypes or to be free of prejudice. You might be influenced by judgments of family or classmates. You could read books or hear speakers who give only one view. Or you could make quick judgments about people's behavior, deciding they are good or bad according to *your* values.

Suppose you hear one of your parents say, "That guy down the street is a slob. He shuffles when he walks and he looks messy. He's always working on junk cars in his drive. But what can you expect from *hillbillies?* They don't ever clean up! I wish they'd move out and we'd get some decent people in the neighborhood."

Maybe you talked to the guy down the street and he seemed friendly enough. You might have seen him all dressed up one day, walking briskly along the sidewalk. Still, you'd remember the judgment: "He's a slob." Maybe you would think every person who works on junk cars is a slob. Or you might decide all people who look and walk like your neighbor are not decent. They don't live as your family;

Even without seeing their faces, you could read the body language of these two. The silent messages of posture tell you that the man is probably advising or comforting the boy. And for proof, all you have to do is look at the next picture. The boy's face shows he's listening intently, and lovingly, to his father's advice.

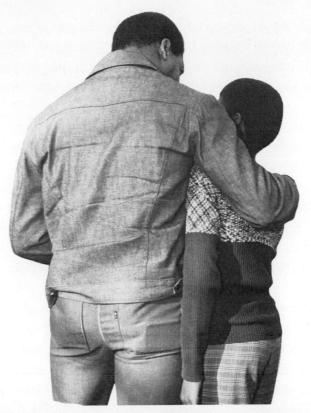

they don't do the things which your family considers good or proper. It doesn't matter that the other guy might have a different idea about what is good and what is proper. The impression has been made and the seeds for the stereotype planted.

Even so, you don't have to "close the book" on people. There are more and more opportunities to learn to read people correctly and avoid false impressions of others.

Social studies in elementary and secondary schools often emphasize causes for certain behavior—why people act as they do. Maybe you have discovered how behavior is related to environment and one's inherited traits. Possibly you have taken part in a classroom role play or sociodrama that teaches how people behave in certain situations.

If you begin to put this type of information together with your new knowledge of body language, you'll get a more complete picture of what people are *really* like. All of that can lead to better communication and understanding—especially if others read you as well as you read them!

TEN
GET YOUR MESSAGE ACROSS

Almost everyone wants to be understood, to communicate with someone. And true communication is more than passing information back and forth. It's a means by which you can establish a relationship with someone—get to know another and let that person get to know you.

While you have been concentrating on the various forms of body language—reading the visible behavior of others—maybe you have also thought about your own silent messages. How do your gestures, facial expressions, postures, and so on affect others? Do people seem to approve of you? Are you easy to get along with? Or do others tend to avoid you? Are there times when you wish you could be more expressive? Do you envy people who are able to attract admirers wherever they go?

In short, what kind of image do you project with your body talk? Sometimes you can get an idea of how others see you by standing in front of a mirror. Of course, your reflection will give you information such as whether your face is clean or if your clothes are in order. But look again. You might see more.

If you stand in a normal fashion—without posing—you should be able to read a message from your posture. Do you think well of yourself? Then you are likely to stand tall, chin up, head slightly back. Do you have doubts about whether people like you? Maybe you'll slouch before the mirror. Do you smile quite a bit? Possibly you find life is pleasant and people fun to be with. Do you have trouble figuring out what to do with your hands? You might twist them nervously or bite your nails or pick at your face because you are unsure of yourself, especially when others are around.

How do you hold yourself in groups? Do you avoid looking at people? Do you sit relaxed, eyes alert, with a look of openness?

What about with your own family? Are you considered the "sourpuss" or smiley member of the household?

You could go on and on with the questions. As you look at yourself, maybe you will want to change a few things. Naturally, you are stuck with the color of your eyes and hair, body structure, and other inherited physical traits. But you can develop different types of postures, facial expressions, and gestures, without being a fake or using cover-ups.

You've already discovered that a good many body signals are given without your conscious thought. However, awareness of body language allows you to control part of this communication process. Just as you learn better speaking methods to make yourself more appealing to others or to put across verbal messages, so you can also learn some body language in order to improve your silent means of expression.

Many doctors believe that people who develop positive body signals and healthy bodies also develop as self-assured and constructive individuals. In other words, if you take care of your physical self (with exercise, good diet, and so on) and practice the body language of a self-confident person, it will help you to become that kind of individual.

Naturally, you aren't going to stand in front of the mirror for hours to do your rehearsing. There are other ways to increase your silent vocabulary—and have fun doing it.

Charades, body talk card games now on the market, and other group activities that make use of pantomime are a big help. Games without words force you to use actions and facial movements to communicate everything from emotions like love and concern to various physical conditions and ideas.

Dance classes, sports, taking part in plays and skits, debate teams, school councils, and a number of other group functions can also help you use your body talk effectively. You'll learn to speak with movements, or support your words with gestures.

Don't pass up opportunities to try out body language when you are doing household errands or on a school field trip. For example, use a smile as you ask for something in a store, or show interest when you listen to someone. Then watch for reactions from others.

Wherever you find opportunities to communicate with others, allow your facial features, hands, arms, body movements and positions to have their "say." Don't be afraid to experiment. Kinesics is not yet an exact science. What you discover about your silent messages could be just as valid as applying scientific theories about body language to your behavior.

You can check out your body clues and cues by observing how others relate or react to you. Also, you can evaluate how expressive you are through body language and whether your silent messages help you communicate.

The checklist that follows is only meant to give you a general picture of what your body says about you. Each question is to be answered with a "Never," "Sometimes," or "Always." Take out a sheet of paper and a pencil to keep track of your responses. A guide to analyzing your own body talk may be found following the questions.

Check Your Clues and Cues

1. When you tell an exciting story, do you use a lot of gestures?

2. In a church or temple, would you try to attract a friend's attention with a hearty wave?

3. When you are listening to someone, do you watch that person's face?

4. Would you smile or nod or use some gesture to encourage a friend who is speaking before a group?

5. If a new student came into your class, would you smile or nod to welcome him or her?

6. Do you signal that you are going to speak by standing or making some noticeable body movement?

7. Do you try to "stare a person down" when you are angry with him or her?

8. With a group of strangers, do you try to let people know with a facial expression or some gestures that you want to be friendly?

9. Do you gesture in some fashion when you are trying to emphasize or make a point in conversation?

10. If someone in your family were hurt, would you use some kind of touch to comfort him or her?

11. Would you elbow or shove your way through a large crowd to see a favorite sports or screen star?

12. When meeting an adult, do you like to shake hands?

13. When people your own age are forming a line, do you try to be at or near the front?

14. If you were going to sit around a table with people of your own age, would you take the chair at the head of the table?

15. In a classroom, would you prefer to sit near the front of the room?

16. Do you stand "at ease" when you are giving a report to a class?

17. Sitting on a crowded bench, would you move aside to make room for a stranger?

18. Would you cover up your dislike for going to the dentist to help a little child overcome a fear of dentists?

19. If you were a sales person, would you put on a happy face in order to get a customer to buy?

20. Do you like to try out different facial expressions and postures in front of a mirror?

21. At parties or during group activities, do you like to mimic comedians or other famous performers?

22. Do you like to demonstrate or *show* a young child a skill such as how to tie a shoe or ride a bike?

23. Would you be one of the first to approach a person whose behavior and looks were very different from yours?

24. When someone doesn't understand you, do you try to *show,* as well as tell, him or her what you mean?

Twenty to twenty-four "Never" answers could mean you need to add more positive, open movements to your silent vo-

cabulary in order to communicate more effectively with others. If most of your answers were "Sometimes" your body language is probably as expressive as the average person's. If you have fifteen to twenty "Always" answers, then it's likely you are an open and maybe aggressive person; your body talk definitely helps you get your messages across!

ABOUT THE AUTHOR

KATHLYN GAY was born in Zion, Illinois, and attended Northern Illinois University and the University of Chicago. She has written many fine books for young people, and has been involved in several innovative educational projects. Ms. Gay now lives with her husband in the Chicago area.